Facts About The Brown Pelican

By Lisa Strattin

© 2016 Lisa Strattin

D1396906

Facts for Kids Picture Books by Lisa Strattin

Anaconda Python, Vol 11

Angora Rabbits, Vol 12

Blue and Gold Macaw, Vol 13

Brown Recluse Spider, Vol 14

American Coot, Vol 15

Spix Macaw, Vol 16

Blue Catfish, Vol 17

Burrowing Owl, Vol 18

California Sea Lion, Vol 19

Capybara, Vol 20

Caracal, Vol 21

Chuckwalla, Vol 22

Hyacinth Macaw, Vol 23

Sign Up for New Release Emails Here

http://lisastrattin.com/subscribe-here

Table of Contents

COLOR ME

INTRODUCTION

Brown Pelican also known as the Pelecanus Occidentalis is mostly found at the coastal areas of southern and westerns untied states. It is one of the most prominent birds found there with their very own representation; collectivity there are only three species of pelican can be found in the westerns hemisphere and the brown pelican is one of the two out all the three that is able to dive into water. Just like the other Pelican, it does have the signature long bill that is around 28 cm to 34.8 cm and really helpful for the Pelican when encountered with the prey while hunting.

COLOR ME

The head is mostly while but in adult pelican it could be a little yellowish, the bill is mostly gray and dark brown from the top but sometimes could have the color variations like rusty hue. The adult pelicans have the blackish brown breast and belly while their feet are totally black, on the other hand the juvenile too look like the same but have brownish grey neck and white underpants. This difference of color combination helps to identify the difference in between the age and maturity of the bird. Due to this color variation and size brown pelican could be easily distinguish between the American White Pelican.

COLOR ME

CHARACTERISTICS AND HABITS

Pelicans are commonly very gregarious birds that prefer to hang around with flock and do have some good coordination with other animals on general and normal basis. They prefer to live in the moderate environment that provide them enough facilities of life like food, environmental settings for nesting, weather conditions and many others. Normally the Brown Pelicans do have a habit of migration from one place to the other in order to get the favorable conditions for living and breeding most of the time. In winters they use to move towards the north coast to get some warmer environment and soothing living conditions that are favorable for them in general.

COLOR ME

LIFE CYCLE

Pelicans use to build their nest in colonies and their nesting is at peak during March and April. Generally they build nest colonies either on tress, bushes or on land as well. The nests are made up of reeds, grasses, straw and sticks. The young Pelican gets hatched in about 2 to 3 days and do not have a single feather on them at that time. that this stag both parents take great care of the new born and feed him for about 35 day until he is not able to walk on land independently. in case of the tree nesting the Pelican do not leave the nest until the 88 days of life at the maximum level.

COLOR ME

Collectively for about 8 to 10 months the young Brown Pelican is under care of the parent pair and get fed by them. At the age of 2 to 5 years normally a Brown Pelican could become sexually mature and become the part of life cycle.

SIZE

Brown Pelican is the smallest one out of all collective eight species of pelican, the total length of a normal pelican is from 106 cm to 137 cm and the average weight is around 2.75 kg to 5.5 kg. The weight of a normal Pelican is enough to be balanced while flying, diving or walking on the land normally. While

COLOR ME

flying the Pelican turns the bill inwards and bends down the neck in order to be more stable and stable while flying.

HABITAT

Mostly you can witness the Pelicans at the southern and western sea coasts in abundance where they live in the flocks of both genders together. Normally they live on land and fly in the air but conditionally to have their food they could dive into water as well. These are really very selective when it is about their living environment, most of the habitats of the Pelican could be found near the seas coasts or water lands as well.

COLOR ME

They are provided with abundance of food at these places that becomes ad good package for them in general. Generally, they like to live at a specified place whole their life but could migrate to any other suitable condition if there is a need of it as well. The highlighted locations of their presence are Atlantic Coast, Gulf Coast, Gulf of Mexico, and Pacific Ocean, British Columbia to South central Chile including Galapagos Islands.

COLOR ME

DIET

Generally, Brown Pelican use to have fishes as their preferred diet and they are not so much selective in them at large. Any fish that could be easily caught by them is their favorite diet and majorly they do not go for the commercially fished species. Apart from that their all time favorite and hit target are pigfish, pinfish, herring, sheepshead, silversides, mullet and minnows. Sometimes other than fish Pelican also go for the other options like crustaceans usually prawns. The daily dies of an adult Pelican is around 1.8 kb that is almost 4.0lb. To full fill the daily intake need of food Pelican do make a lot of attempts at the coastal areas and sometimes do relay on the alternate diet options.

COLOR ME

SUITABILITY AS PETS

Having a Brown Pelican as your pet is such an imaginary thing that could hit your mind, it is a free bird that likes to live in groups and fly according to the environmental conditions and mood too. Having it bound in to a limited field is simply not suitable for them at all. The Pelican is not able to live in any controlled environment and it could simply put some bad influence on their health too. If you want to have a good bond with Pelican then you could visit them with regularity, feed them and spend some good time with them but keeping them at your place or any controlled environment is really not a good idea at all. Their friendly and calm nature will make up a good bond between you and them but never try to restrict them.

COLOR ME

For more Kindle Downloads Visit <u>Lisa Strattin Author Page</u> on Amazon Author Central

http://www.amazon.com/Lisa-Strattin/e/B00DC7L4SK

To see upcoming titles, visit my website at <u>LisaStrattin.com</u> – all books available on kindle!

STUFFED BROWN PELICAN TOY

You can get one by copying and pasting this link into your browser: **http://amzn.to/1rF5L8A**

Made in the USA
Middletown, DE
06 August 2016